CLOUD9

A CHILD'S GUIDE TO GETTING THERE

X-mas 2015

To Abby
From Grandma

Cloud 9
A Child's Guide to Getting There

by Larry Kuhnke

Larry Kuhnke (signature)

Tate Publishing *& Enterprises*

Cloud 9
Copyright © 2011 by Larry Kuhnke. All rights reserved.

No part of this publication may be reproduced, stored in a retrieval system or transmitted in any way by any means, electronic, mechanical, photocopy, recording or otherwise without the prior permission of the author except as provided by USA copyright law.

This novel is a work of fiction. Names, descriptions, entities and incidents included in the story are products of the author's imagination. Any resemblance to actual persons, events and entities is entirely coincidental.

The opinions expressed by the author are not necessarily those of Tate Publishing, LLC.

Published by Tate Publishing & Enterprises, LLC
127 E. Trade Center Terrace | Mustang, Oklahoma 73064 USA
1.888.361.9473 | www.tatepublishing.com

Tate Publishing is committed to excellence in the publishing industry. The company reflects the philosophy established by the founders, based on Psalm 68:11,
"The Lord gave the word and great was the company of those who published it."

Book design copyright © 2011 by Tate Publishing, LLC. All rights reserved.
Cover and interior design by Elizabeth A. Mason
Illustrations by Kurt Jones

Published in the United States of America

ISBN: 978-1-61663-431-5
1. Juvenile Fiction: Concepts: General
2. Juvenile Fiction: General
11.10.19

The 1896 edition of the International Cloud Atlas defined ten types of clouds. The ninth cloud was the cumulonimbus, which rose to a height of 10 km (33,000 feet, or 6 miles). This was the highest cloud. If you are on Cloud 9, you are on top of the world.

This book is dedicated to Mom and Dad. More than anything else they gave me, I most appreciate and treasure their direction, their values, and their unending love—all of which were shown in their life practices.

TABLE OF CONTENTS

Men & Women in Service to Our Country	11
Firefighters, Law Enforcement, & Other Emergency Response People	12
Our Beautiful Country	13
Mothers & Fathers	14
Helping Others & Sharing	17
Education	18
Is There a God?	19
Our Country's Flag	20
Churches & Other Places of Worship	22
Your Conscience	24
Ethics & Morals	25
Your Body	26

SPORTSMANSHIP	28
HOLIDAYS	29
ENGLISH LANGUAGE	31
MANNERS	32
YOUR WORD	33
GOALS	34
YOUR FAMILY	36
LOYALTY	38
DREAMS	39
LAUGHTER	41
WONDER	42
TAKING CARE OF YOUR THINGS	43
CHORES	45
FINANCIAL ACCOUNTABILITY	46
HUMANITY	48
CONVICTIONS	49
PATIENCE	51
RESPONSIBILITY	52
ATTITUDE	52

Role Models	55
Friends	56
Habits	58
Safety	59
Sing & Dance	60
The Truth	62
Integrity	63
History	65
Government	66
Independence	67
Winning	68
Time	70
Conclusion	71

CLOUD 9

MEN & WOMEN IN SERVICE TO OUR COUNTRY

These brave people risk their lives to protect our lives and our country. They deserve respect; and when they are in uniform, a salute would be appropriate. You will often hear the hymns of each branch of service. Learn and understand the words to each hymn.

Larry Kuhnke

FIREFIGHTERS, LAW ENFORCEMENT, & OTHER EMERGENCY RESPONSE PEOPLE

These brave people have very dangerous jobs. They enforce our laws, they respond to dangerous situations, and they do their best to keep us safe. Give them the respect they deserve. When they have their sirens on or lights flashing, stay out of their way, as they may be trying to save someone's life. *Be sure you know how to contact emergency response people if and when they are ever needed.*

CLOUD 9

OUR BEAUTIFUL COUNTRY

We have a very beautiful country. It is blessed with many lakes, rivers, mountains, hills, deserts, farmlands, and more. Do your best to keep it clean and to protect the water, animals, trees, and other vegetation that share our country. Appreciate what we have been blessed with; spend time outdoors, enjoying these natural gifts. Learn about the trees, the flowers, the animals, lakes, rivers, streams, and all of our other natural blessings.

Develop good habits for reducing, reusing, and recycling.

ADAGE: "FLOWERS ARE GOD'S WAY OF SMILING ON US."

Larry Kuhnke

MOTHERS & FATHERS

A parent is the best friend you will ever have. At times, it may be difficult to believe this, as you will have disagreements, or you may not understand their reasoning; but as you grow older and mature, you will easily recognize that they had your best interests at heart. Learn to appreciate all that a parent does for you, and respect their instructions and decisions. They know what is best for you. Communicate openly and frequently with them.

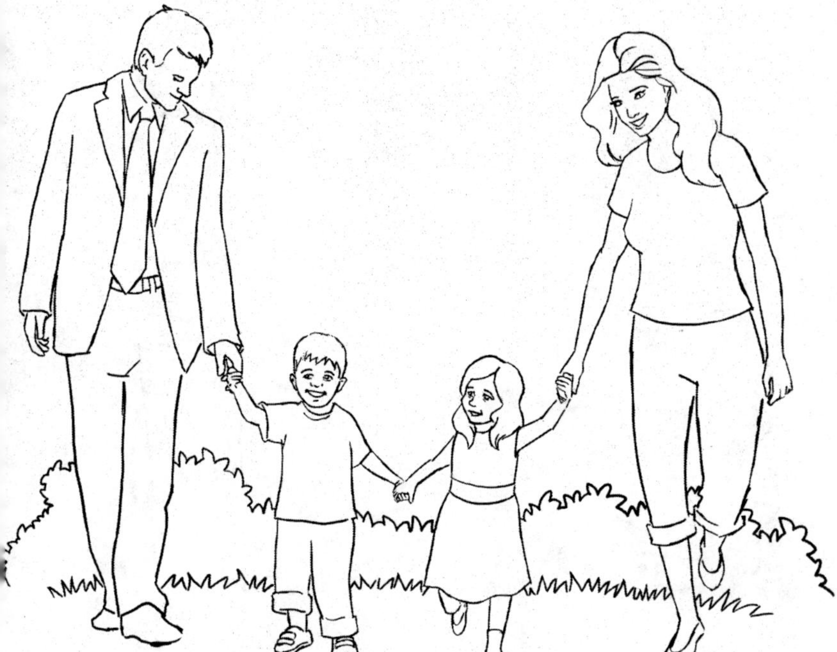

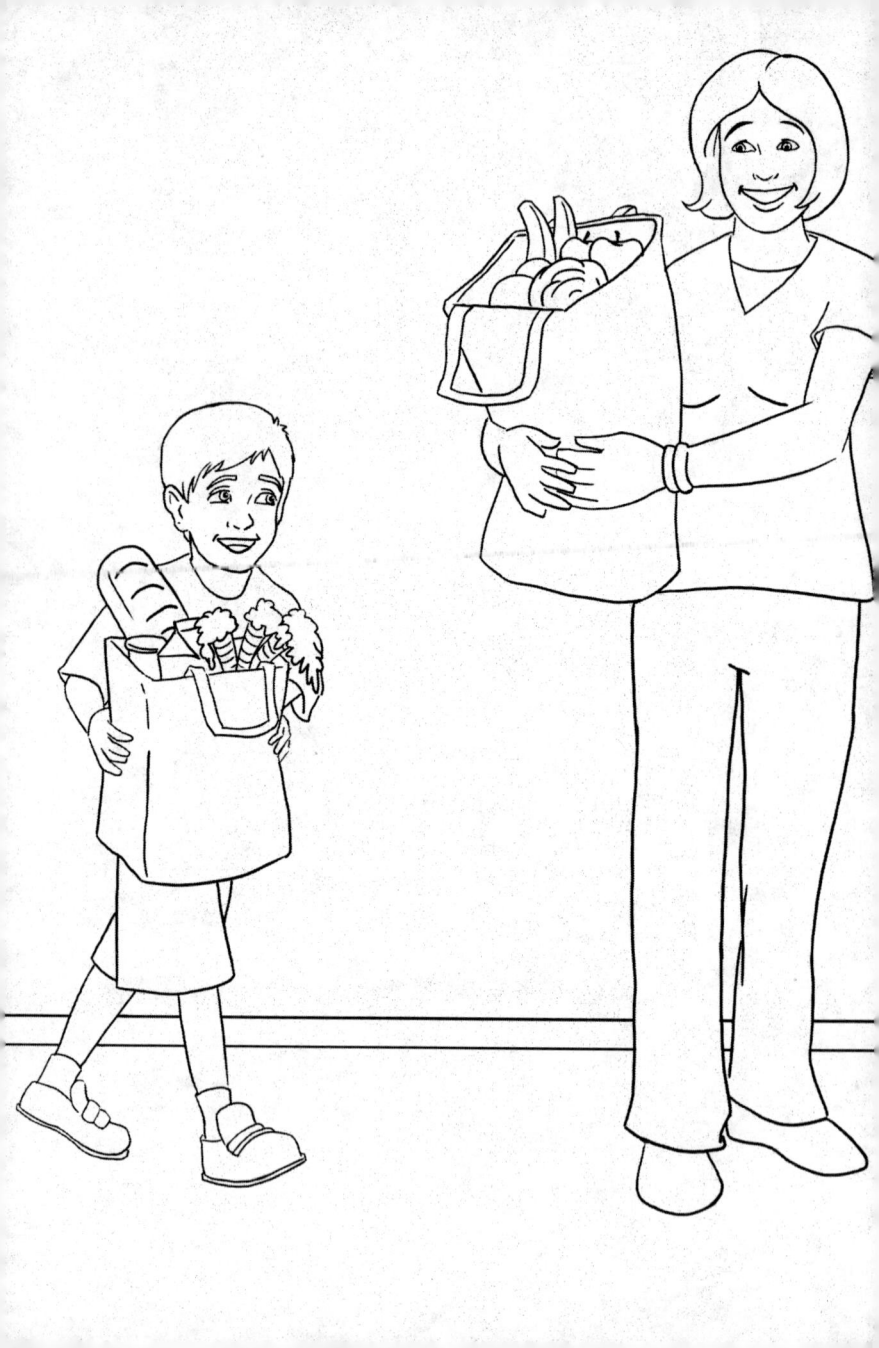

CLOUD 9

HELPING OTHERS & SHARING

Be very thankful that you have been blessed with so many good things. Always do your best to share with and help others. Unlike receiving a gift that may only last a short while, the pleasant memories of giving will remain with you forever. Develop the habit of doing something unexpected every day that will make someone smile.

Larry Kuhnke

EDUCATION

Learning is just as important as the air we breathe. The more we learn, the easier our lives will be. In school and elsewhere, you need to be attentive. It's much easier to learn while you are young than when you grow older. Teachers, parents, and others work very hard trying to teach you things you need to know. You should listen and learn.

> Adage: "When you listen, you learn; when you speak, others learn."

CLOUD 9

IS THERE A GOD?

Look about and answer the question yourself. The complexity of the human body and mind; the solar system; the birds, fish, and animals; the trees and flowers; and so much more—could all of these creations have just happened? Develop your faith by reading the Bible and other spiritual books and talking with others about God. Spend quiet time daily, thanking God for your blessings and seeking guidance through challenging times and with difficult decisions.

Larry Kuhnke

OUR COUNTRY'S FLAG

Our flag is very special. It is the symbol of our wonderful country. Our flag should be treated with respect. Think about our country when you see it. Learn the meaning of the stars, stripes, and colors. Learn the rules for flying the flag, including how to fold it when not being flown. Recite the "Pledge of Allegiance" clearly and sing the "Star-Spangled Banner" proudly.

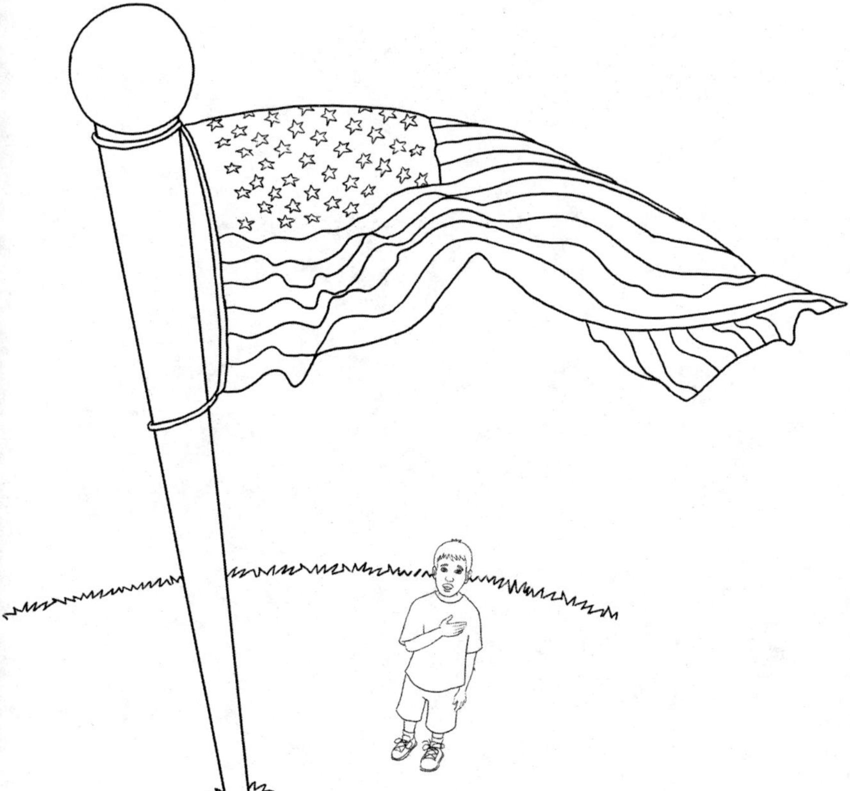

Larry Kuhnke

CHURCHES & OTHER PLACES OF WORSHIP

Churches and other places of worship are where people gather to visit with God and pray. They may be asking for help or spiritual guidance or may be thanking God for their blessings. Also, marriage and death rituals are frequently observed in churches.

Think about this, and say a little prayer whenever you are near one of God's homes.

Larry Kuhnke

YOUR CONSCIENCE

Your conscience is your inner guide. It privately tells you what is right and what is wrong. You should always obey your conscience. It's always there for you.

CLOUD 9

ETHICS & MORALS

If you consistently apply the good behavioral suggestions in this book, you will be considered a person with good ethics and morals; you do things right. You are truthful, you care for others, you work hard, and so forth. Being considered a person with good ethics and morals is one of the highest compliments you could ever hope for. You will be well on your way to Cloud 9.

Larry Kuhnke

YOUR BODY

You only have one body and it is very important to you. If you take good care of it, it will take good care of you. Share your body's secrets only with those you love and trust and those who love, trust, and care about you.

> ADAGE: "AN APPLE A DAY KEEPS THE DOCTOR AWAY."

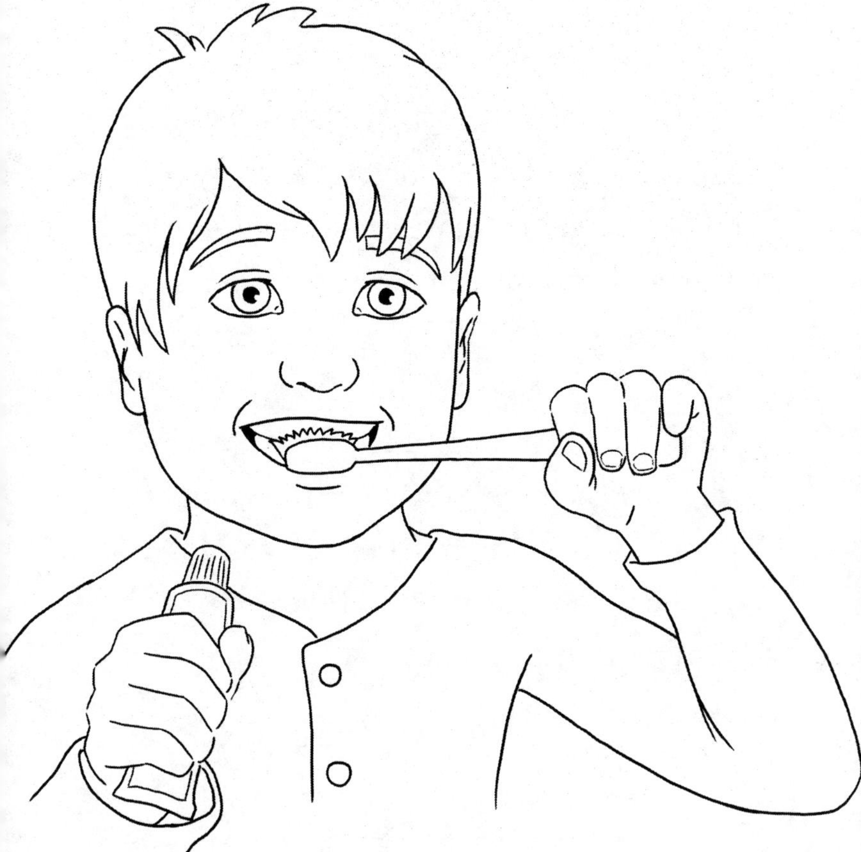

Larry Kuhnke

SPORTSMANSHIP

Sports, games, and other contests are usually fun. Every contest has a winner and a loser. A fast person will likely beat a slower person in a marathon. A stronger person will likely beat a weaker person in lifting weights. Everybody is good at something. Figure out where you can succeed. Whatever the competition, always do your best. If you lose, be gracious to the winner. If you win, be humble and thankful.

ADAGE: "IT'S NOT WHETHER YOU WIN OR LOSE, BUT HOW YOU PLAY THE GAME."

CLOUD 9

HOLIDAYS

Learn and appreciate the meaning for every holiday. There may be holidays that you do not participate in, but respect the rights of others to observe those holidays.

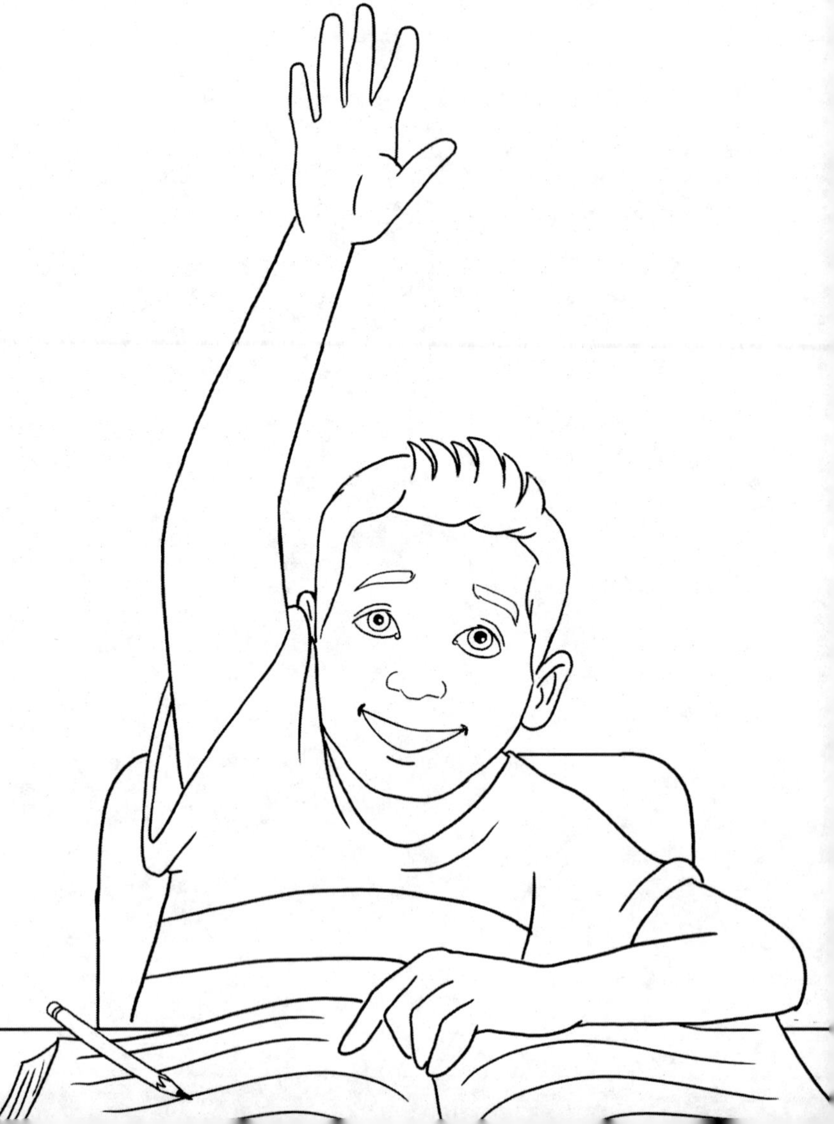

CLOUD 9

ENGLISH LANGUAGE

Reading, writing, and speaking the English language properly are important to your happiness and success. Learn and use the language well. Choose your words wisely.

Develop a plan for increasing your vocabulary.

Larry Kuhnke

MANNERS

Saying "please" and "thank you" are the most common examples of good manners. Find a reliable source to help you with the development of your good manners. This source may be an authoritative person, a book, or a website.

Using good manners is one of the easiest and quickest ways to earn the respect and affection of adults and others.

CLOUD 9

YOUR WORD

Your word is yours and yours alone. Others will judge you by how you keep your word. If you say you will do something, do it. Keeping your word will keep you at peace with yourself.

Larry Kuhnke

GOALS

Goals in life are important, no matter how big or small. Without goals, it's impossible to measure your progress. Setting, and then achieving, goals is very rewarding.

> ADAGE: "IF IT'S WORTH DOING AT ALL, IT'S WORTH DOING RIGHT."

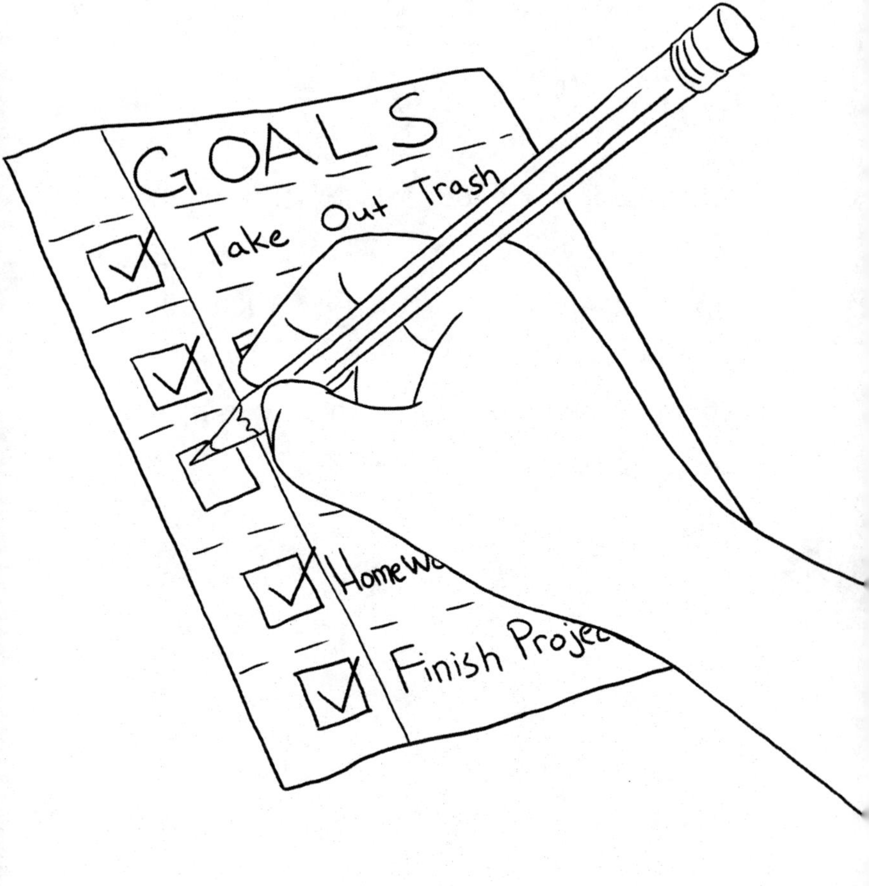
GOALS
Take Out Trash
Homewo
Finish Projec

YOUR FAMILY

The members of your family are very special. They will always be there for you. Spend time with them, love them, get to know them, help them, and protect them. Dinner together with no outside interruptions is very rewarding.

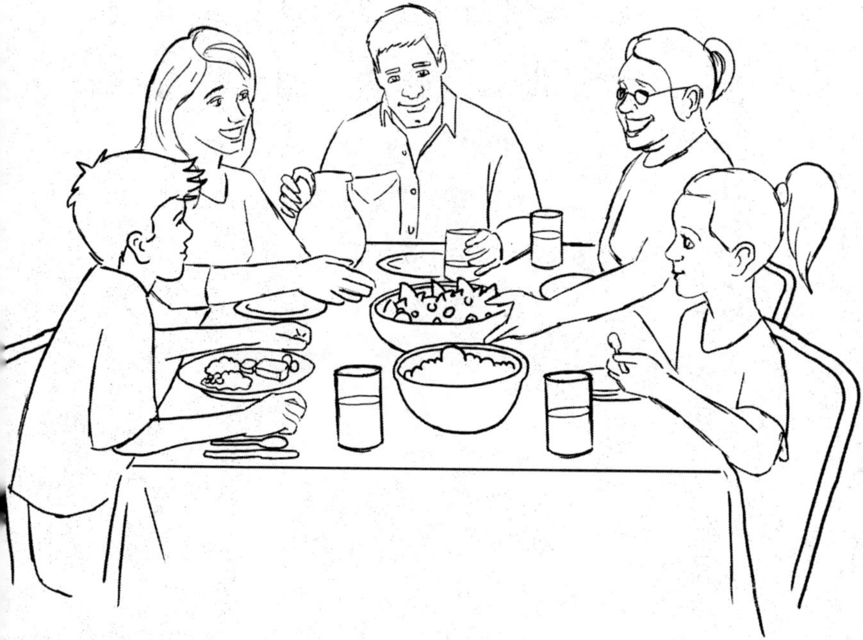

Larry Kuhnke

LOYALTY

Loyalty means being true, faithful, and committed. Be loyal to your family, your friends, your country, and to any groups or organizations to which you belong. When you become employed, be loyal to your employer as well as the others mentioned here. Always give 100 percent or more.

> ADAGE: "UNDERPROMISE AND OVERDELIVER."

CLOUD 9

DREAMS

It's wonderful to dream. And if you have a dream that is of real interest to you, pursue it. If you are persistent, you may make your dream come true. Your favorite songs, your favorite restaurant, airplanes, landing on the moon, electricity, television, computers—at one time, these were nothing more than someone's dream.

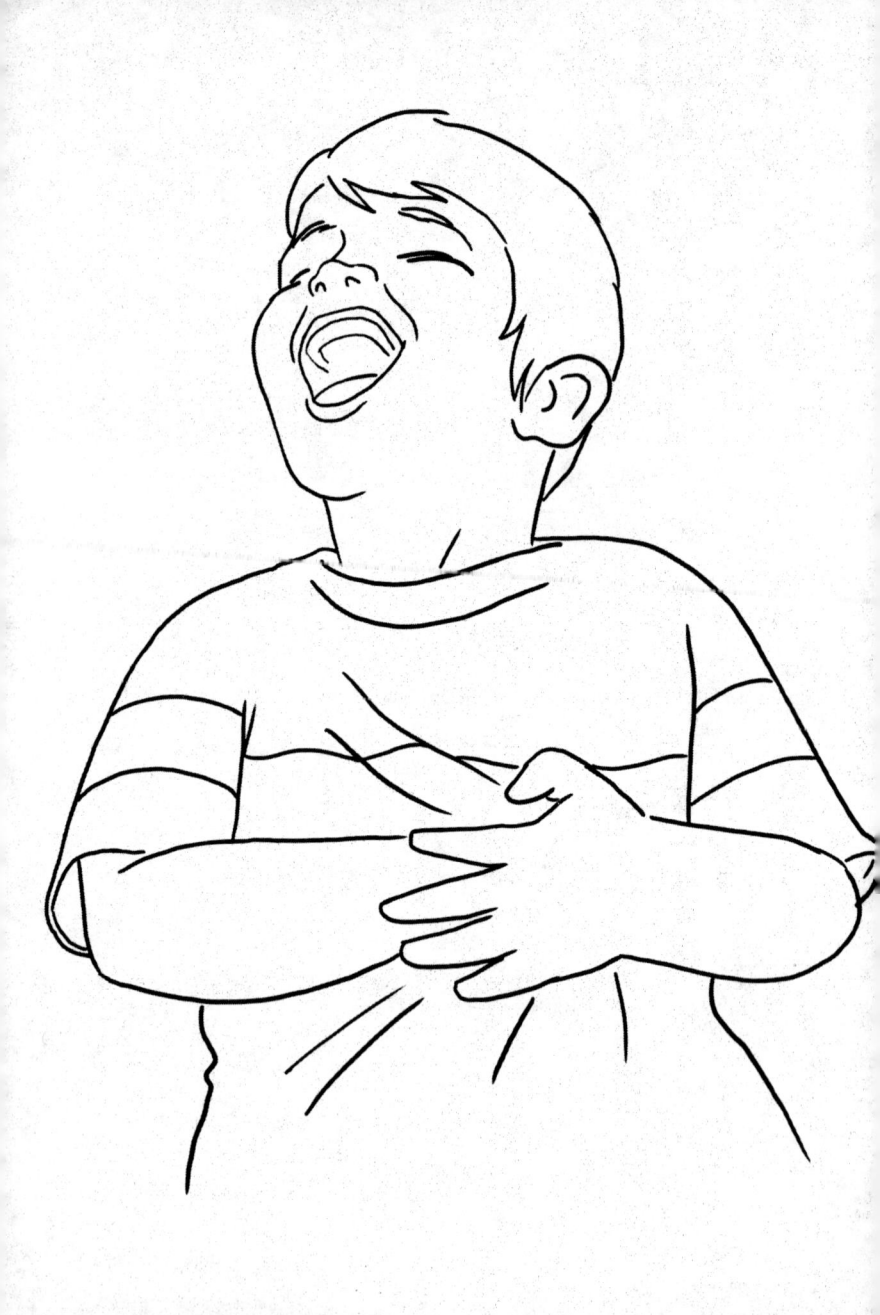

CLOUD 9

LAUGHTER

Laughter is an expression of enjoyment. Many doctors believe that daily laughter will help you live longer. It's important to laugh for the right reasons and at the right times.

Someone else's bad luck or misfortune is not something to be laughed at.

Larry Kuhnke

WONDER

It's exciting to wonder about things. It's even more exciting to explore and learn about the things you wonder about. You will be amazed at how much fun you will have when you know the answers to things you, and so many other people, wonder about.

CLOUD 9

TAKING CARE OF YOUR THINGS

Show your appreciation for what you have by taking care of your things. Clothes, toys, books, hobby materials, and anything else that you have should be put away when not in use. If you take care of your things, they will last longer and you will be able to enjoy them much more. Never use your things for anything other than what they should be used for. Your room, closets, and other storage areas should always be neat.

Adage: "Waste not, want not."

CLOUD 9

CHORES

Properly taking care of your chores in a timely manner is a very good way of thanking your mother and/or father for the many chores they do for you: cooking, washing your clothes, and earning money to pay for your home, your clothes, your food, and other things that you need. Performing your chores will help prepare you for your time in the working world.

> ADAGE: "MANY HANDS MAKE LIGHT WORK."

Larry Kuhnke

FINANCIAL ACCOUNTABILITY

Spend your money wisely, and save as much as possible. If you find it necessary to borrow money, be sure to repay on the agreed terms. Borrowing is a privilege, not a right. Never, ever borrow unless you have a safe plan to repay.

ADAGE: "HOW YOU USE AND MANAGE YOUR MONEY IS MORE IMPORTANT THAN HOW MUCH MONEY YOU HAVE."

Larry Kuhnke

HUMANITY

There is no one like you in this world. Even twins have differences. You will have disagreements with other people, but you should always respect their opinions. Listen with an open mind. Judge other people by your own knowledge of and experiences with them. There are exceptions to this; ask a parent or other responsible adult whom you trust to explain.

Adage: "Do unto others as you would have others do unto you."

Adage: "There are at least two sides to every story."

CLOUD 9

CONVICTIONS

Convictions are deep and well-thought-out beliefs. They are based on what you know to be true about something. Stay with and support your convictions unless you learn something new and of substance that gives you reason to change.

Adage: "Facts and convictions, not feelings and conveniences."

4 feet

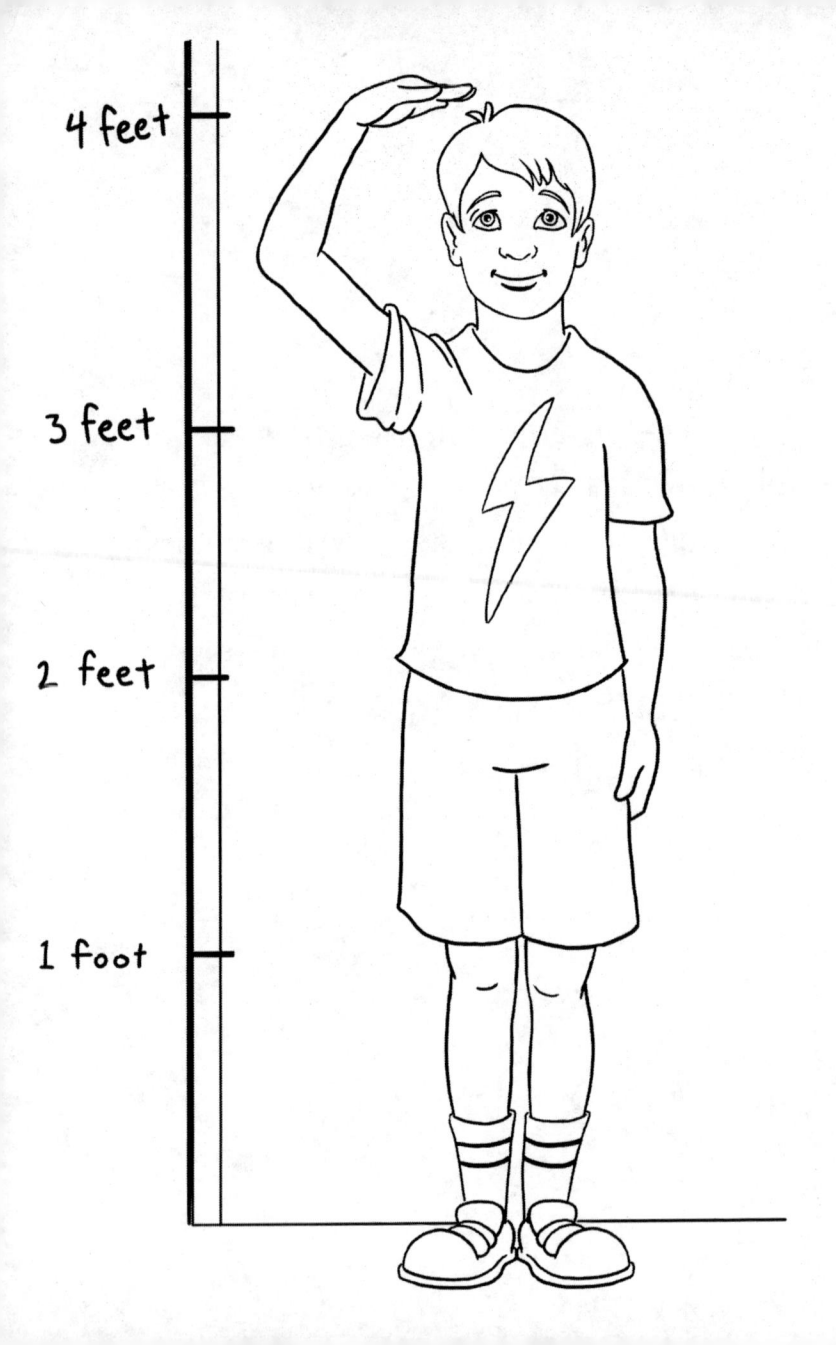

3 feet

2 feet

1 foot

CLOUD 9

PATIENCE

Patience is calmly, and in certain situations, politely, waiting for something to happen; for something to be accomplished; or for someone to respond. *Calmly* is the key word in this explanation. Perhaps you are waiting for a flower to bloom, for your dinner, for a friend to arrive, or perhaps you are trying to solve a puzzle or learn something new. Patience is a lifesaver; it will minimize the stress in your life. Stress is very unhealthy. Learn about stress, and find ways to keep it out of your life.

Larry Kuhnke

RESPONSIBILITY

You are responsible for your actions and your inactions. Consider whether the results of your action or inaction will be good or bad. When you make mistakes, learn from them. A parent or someone else who loves you may assist you when you are younger; but as you become an adult, you will have to assume full responsibility.

ATTITUDE

The longer you live, the more you will realize the impact of your attitude on your life. Attitude is more important

CLOUD 9

than the facts. It is more important than the past; than education; than money; than circumstances; than failures; than successes; and more important than what other people think, say, or, do. It is more important than talent or skills. It can make or break a person, a friendship, a family, a team, or a business.

The remarkable thing is that you have a choice every day regarding the attitude you will embrace. You cannot change the past or the fact that other people will act in their own way. You cannot change the inevitable. But you can control your attitude.

Life is 10 percent what happens to you and 90 percent how you react to it.

CLOUD 9

ROLE MODELS

Role models are special people. They are the ones who do something in a manner that sets them favorably apart from others. He or she may be a teacher who is able to help you learn; he or she may be a baseball player who takes the time to sign autographs; or he or she may be a friend who really looks after you. If you have a role model, be sure to tell him or her. Live your life in a manner that will make you a role model for others.

Larry Kuhnke

FRIENDS

Friends are very special. They are the ones who are there for you in good times and bad. Choose your friends wisely. They should like you, and you should like them—not for what they have, where they live, or what they give you, but for who they are.

ADAGE: "THE ROAD TO A FRIEND'S HOUSE IS NEVER LONG."

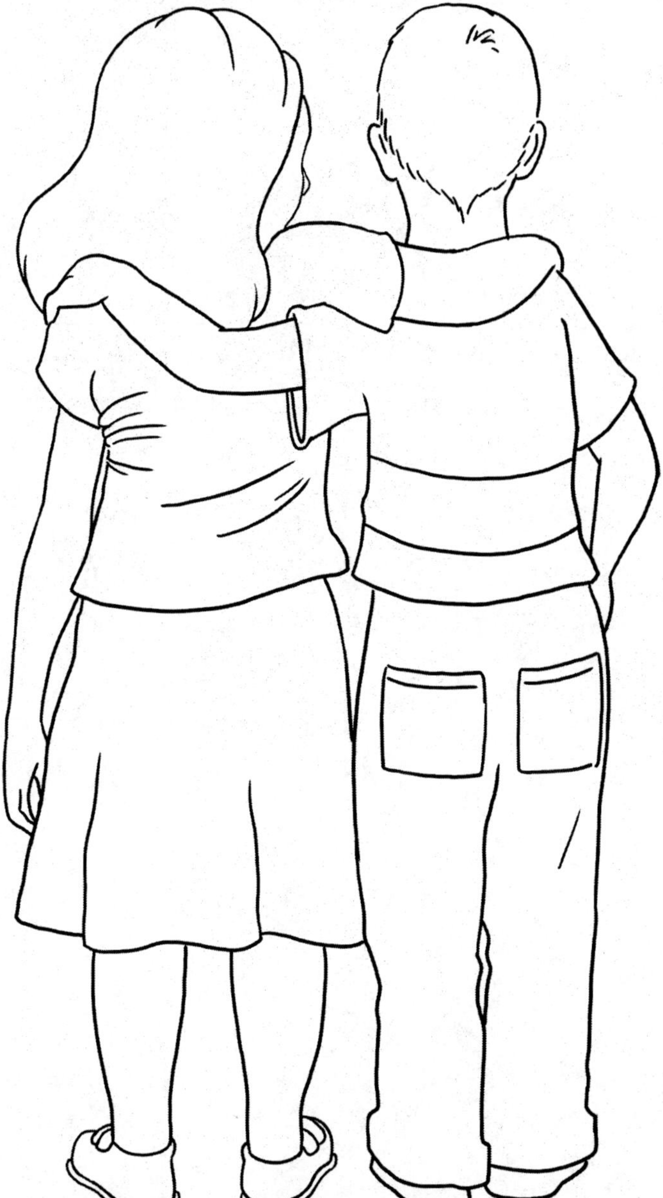

Larry Kuhnke

HABITS

It is very easy and so worthwhile to develop good habits. Habits are "savers." A good habit may save you time, it may save you from frustration, it may save you from illness, or it may save you from losing something of value. Good habits will prevent you from developing bad habits, which are very difficult to break.

Adage: "Why is there always time to do it over but seldom time to do it right the first time?"

ADAGE: "HASTE MAKES WASTE."

CLOUD 9

SAFETY

Look for, think about, and avoid dangers that may injure you, your family, or friends as well your home or other things of value to you. No one can do more to keep you safe than you yourself can do.

ADAGE: "BETTER SAFE THAN SORRY."

Larry Kuhnke

SING & DANCE

Singing and dancing may be the expressions of a culture, an emotion, a tradition, a special event, or maybe just for fun. Be comfortable singing and dancing. Chances are you will be able to do both as well as most of your friends. Singing and dancing will bring years of fun, and they are great ways to meet new people.

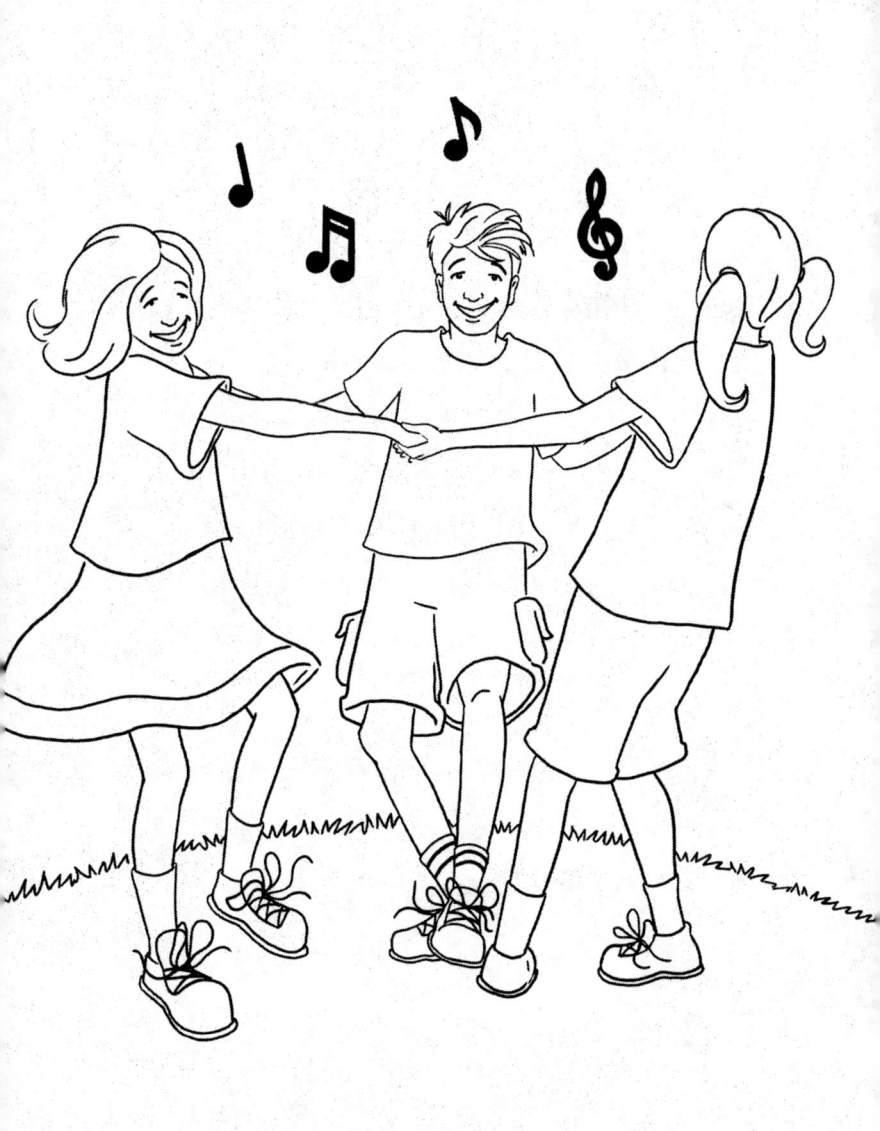

Larry Kuhnke

THE TRUTH

Telling the truth isn't always easy, but it is the right thing to do. Sometimes it is even painful, but knowing that you have always told the truth will make you feel good. The people who know you will trust you, and that is a very good thing.

> Adage: "The truth will set you free."

CLOUD 9

INTEGRITY

Peace of mind is not found in who others think you are but in who you really are.

Are you the same person around your family and friends as you are when you are alone?

ADAGE: "IT'S LONELY AT THE TOP."

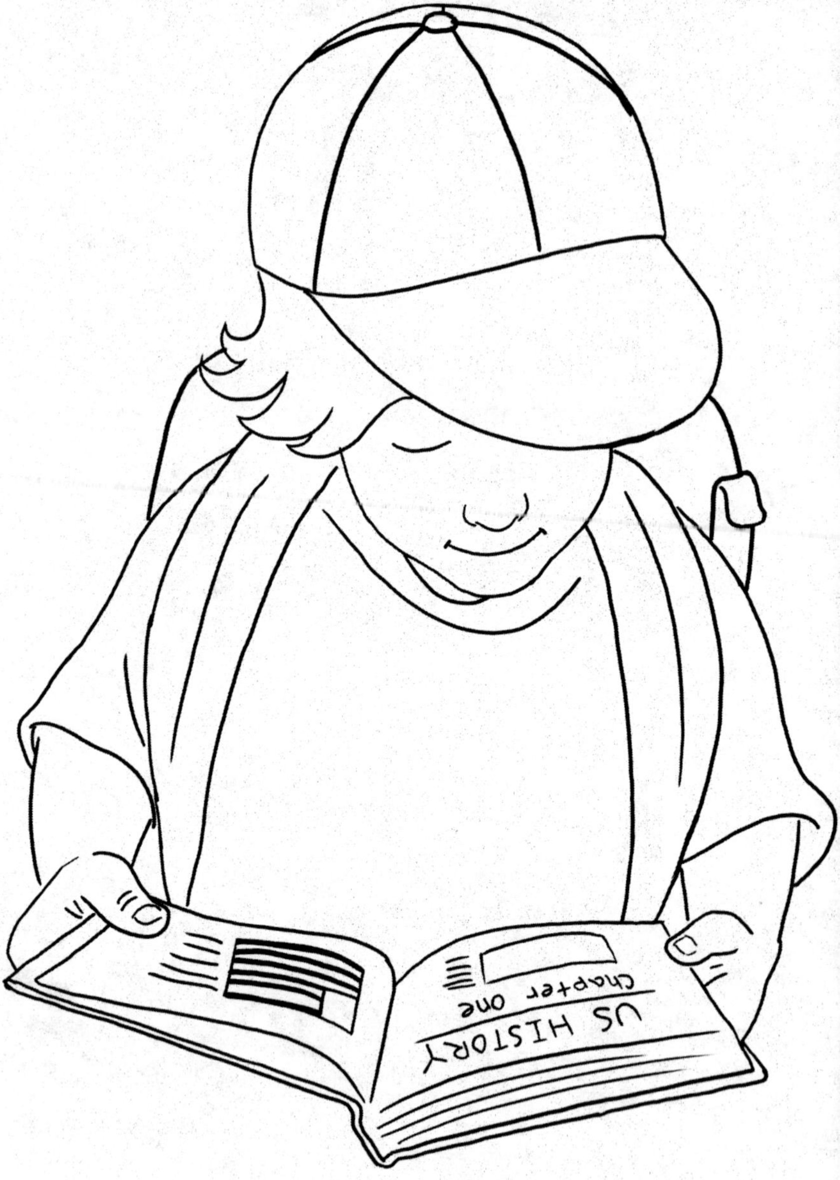
US HISTORY
Chapter one

CLOUD 9

HISTORY

You will find the history of your community, state, and country very interesting. Learn all you can. So much of history is fascinating. It will be fun to share this knowledge with friends and family.

Larry Kuhnke

GOVERNMENT

Learn how your local, state, and national governments work. Read and understand the Declaration of Independence, the Constitution, and the Bill of Rights. When you are of age, become active. Prior to voting, know your candidates and what they stand for; research and understand ballot issues.

CLOUD 9

INDEPENDENCE

Independence is one of the most useful gifts you can give to yourself. The less dependent you are on other people, the more control you will have over your own life. Learn to tie your shoes; to prepare your own snacks; to wash, fold and iron your clothes; and to fix things that break.

Larry Kuhnke

WINNING

A favorite adage of mine: "Winning isn't everything. It's the only thing."

No one can win at everything, but everyone can win at something. Recognize your weaknesses and your strengths. Do your best in your weaker areas, and be the best in your stronger areas. Winning is not just about sports, team, or individual competitions; it's about the components of life. You may be a winner by simply achieving a personal goal you set for yourself.

ADAGE: "WHEN THE GOING GETS TOUGH, THE TOUGH GET GOING."

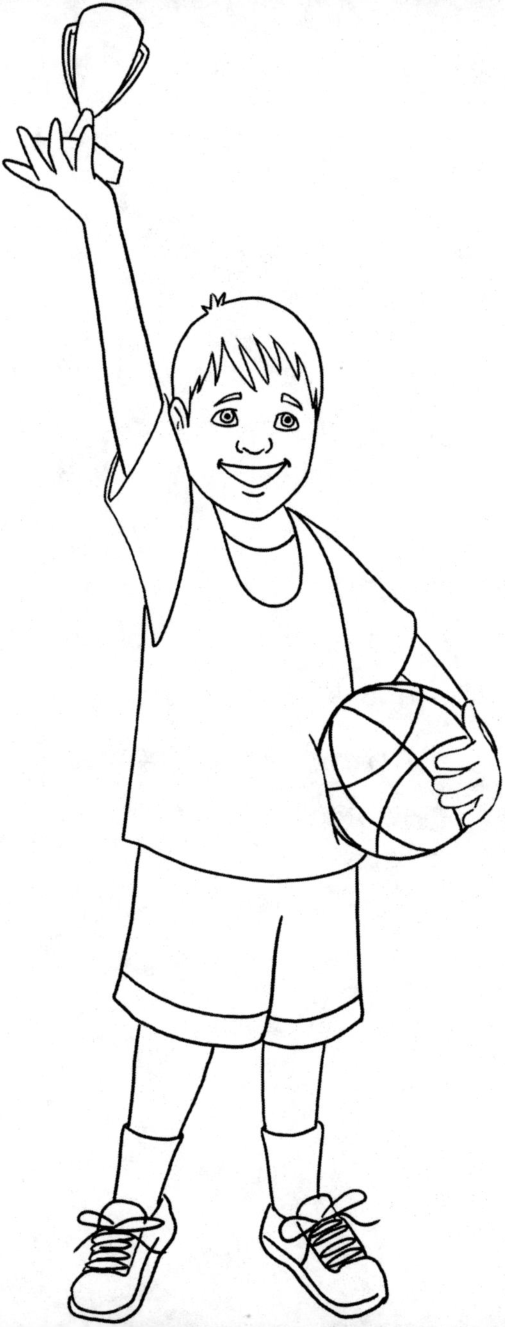

Larry Kuhnke

TIME

At your young age, it is hard to comprehend and appreciate the value of time. As you grow older, time will be much more meaningful to you. Always make the best of the time you have. Some of us enjoy long lives with a lot of time; some are not so lucky.

> ADAGE: "TOMORROW IS PROMISED TO NO ONE."

CLOUD 9

CONCLUSION

In closing, I would like to share with you three favorite readings of mine:

THE SERENITY PRAYER

God grant me the serenity to accept the things I cannot change, the courage to change the things I can, and the wisdom to know the difference.

Larry Kuhnke

FOOTPRINTS

One night, a man had a dream. He dreamed he was walking along the beach with the Lord. Across the sky flashed scenes from his life. For each scene, he noticed two sets of footprints in the sand; one belonged to him and the other to the Lord. When the last scene of his life flashed before him, he looked back at the footprints in the sand. He noticed that many times along the path of his life, there was only one set of footprints. He also noticed that it happened at the very lowest and saddest times in his life. This really bothered him, and he questioned the Lord about it. "Lord, you said that once I decided to follow you, you'd walk with me all the way. But I noticed that during the most troublesome times in my life, there is only one set of footprints. I

CLOUD 9

don't understand why when I needed you most you would leave me."

The Lord replied, "My son, my precious child, I love you and would never leave you. During your times of trial and suffering, when you see only one set of footprints, it was then that I carried you."

Larry Kuhnke

"COMMON SENSE"
An Excerpt from a Speech Delivered by President Abraham Lincoln

You cannot bring about prosperity by discouraging thrift. You cannot strengthen the weak by weakening the strong. You cannot help small men by tearing down big men. You cannot help the poor by destroying the rich. You cannot lift the wage earner by pulling down the wage payer. You cannot keep out of trouble by spending more than your income. You cannot further the brotherhood of man by inciting class hatred. You cannot establish sound security on borrowed money. You cannot build character and courage by taking away a man's initiative and independence. You

CLOUD 9

cannot help men permanently by doing for them what they could and should do for themselves.

ABOUT THE AUTHOR

I came from a very humble upbringing. My father, for most of his life after service in the United States Marine Corps, worked for Ford Motor Company. My mother worked part-time in a tavern. I am the second of five children. For most of my life, we lived in a three-bedroom house with only one bathroom, which we also shared with a maternal grandmother who lived with us. I married at the age of twenty and had to borrow five hundred dollars to set up our home. My family and I enjoyed good reputations and I was able to borrow the money from a bank on just my signature.

I now have two daughters and four

grandchildren. My daughters are healthy, happy, respected, and successful. I hope and pray that my grandchildren and other children have the same opportunities for happiness and success that I enjoyed.

Hopefully, this book will help them.

As I wrote this book, I was blessed with many pleasant childhood memories. I continue to be blessed with the cherished love of young children. The mutual affection that I enjoy with younger children is special and was the motivating force behind my writing this book.